THE TRUTH ABOUT SELLING

D1202979

Edited by Jocelyn Carbonara
Designed by Tom Howey

ISBN 978-1-7366249-0-6

THE TRUTH ABOUT SELLING

*How to influence others to invest
in your ideas, products, and services*

JOHN H. THALHEIMER

Part Fable and Part Instruction Manual, this book provides insights on how to get others to invest in your ideas, products, and service. First, we follow our hero Johnny as he tries to sell his latest product at The Small Business International Market, competing with thousands of other vendors. With Johnny, we discover how hard it can be to bring your product to market and what you need to do to be successful. In the second part of the book, we learn the knowledge, actions, and techniques we need to use to get others to invest in our idea, product, or service. Each chapter includes Questions to Ask of Yourself and Exercises to Improve your Selling Technique. Designed to guide entrepreneurs, small business owners, and organizational leaders to achieve marketing success.

Marla–
thanks for saying yes
to the adventure

Contents

I stand on the shoulders of giants who,
without, I would never touch the sky.
Small and large, you have lifted me.

The Story
Behind the Story

I never thought I would be a salesperson. In a college marketing class, my professor said, "We are all salespeople," and I scoffed out loud. I did not need to sell anything. I was an operations manager, focused on efficiency. To me, most salespeople were sleazy, fast-talking, money-hungry individuals who cared more about achieving their goals than helping people.

In my life's journey, I learned that the professor was right. "We are all salespeople." Selling is influencing another person to invest their money, time, energy, prestige in our products, services, and ideas. Sales can be as simple as persuading someone to go to the movies with us or as complicated as landing a significant contract with a Fortune 500 company. Selling happens at home, at work, and on social media. It happens between coworkers, family members, even strangers.

Selling is a skill that we all need to develop, but it is essential for entrepreneurs who are working to take their business to the next level. Or business owners whose company sales have stalled under a million dollars. Or organizational leaders who are trying to implement new, innovative ideas in a conservative corporation that is slow to adopt change.

As I made the transition from a senior operations leader in a large corporation to an entrepreneur, selling and marketing became my Achilles heel. Like Kevin Costner in *Field of Dreams*, I thought if I built it, they would come. But I learned this is not true. Selling is work. It takes learning. It takes planning. It takes effort. I made a lot of mistakes before I learned how to influence others to invest in me and my services; before I learned to sell.

I designed this book to teach you how to get others to invest in your ideas, products, or services. The first section is a fable, where we follow our hero, Johnny, as he learns how to sell his product in an open market. The second section covers the knowledge, actions, and techniques you will need to get others to invest in your idea, product, or service successfully. Within each section of the second part of the book, I have included Questions to Ask and *Exercises to Improve Your Technique* to help you reflect and practice the techniques discussed.

Say it with me...

I am a salesperson.

And my journey to success starts today.

Enjoy,

John

Johnny Goes to The Market

Johnny's Quest
for Better Sales

Johnny opened the door to the largest market he had ever seen. Like an ancient Egyptian market, the great hall stretched out before him with hundreds and hundreds of vendor booths of all shapes and sizes. Salespeople, technicians, artists, and their helpers darted from one stall to the next, preparing for the opening day of The Small Business International Market, less than forty-eight hours away.

The Small Business International Market seemed to be the best conference to sell Johnny's product. He had researched and learned it was ten-days long, and hundreds of thousands of small business owners, general managers, executives, and human resources professionals would be there.

As Johnny stepped inside, a cacophony noise from all the activity reached Johnny's ears.

"Vendor number?" a distant voice asked.

"Huh?"

"Your vendor number, so I can tell you where to set up."

Johnny looked at the lady holding a clipboard as if she were speaking a language he hadn't learned. He had worked very hard to bring his product to this particular market because of its history of turning new vendors into millionaires. If everything went well, his life would change for the better.

But he wasn't off to the best start, because he was twelve hours late.

Johnny told the lady with the clipboard his vendor number. She quickly spat out a section and booth number for him to set up within.

"Everything you requested and shipped will be there. If not, look for one of the vendor ambassadors in the blue shirts, and they will help you."

"What's your vendor number?" The clipboard lady had quickly turned to those queued up behind Johnny.

Johnny navigated the aisle looking for his section. Hundreds of people scurried back and forth, as if he had just entered an ants' nest. Some were carrying ladders, pushing carts, or standing still and holding coffee. Others pointed and yelled.

The booths ranged from corporate professional to mom-and-pop chic. As Johnny walked through the chaos of late-day set-up, he wondered if both his stall and product would stand out. He had spent a good portion of his savings to be there; and if it didn't work... Well, he didn't want to think about that.

This dream had all started two years ago when he had an idea that would revolutionize his field. He had developed the prototype in his home office and then started to show it to a select group of individuals to see what they thought. All of them had said it was a game-changer.

For most of his adult life, Johnny had led teams in various industries. And no matter where he worked, employee performance management was always a challenge. In some cases, his colleagues did not know the first thing about employment management. In some cases, a company had inconsistency in how an employee's performance was managed, or its managers struggled to find time to converse with their teams about performance.

Johnny realized that if he created a systematic approach to employee performance management that catered to struggling middle managers and human resource professionals, business performance would improve exponentially. After a night of star watching, he named it the True Star Performance Management System™ (TSPMS).

After twenty years, Johnny then decided to leave the corporate life behind and chase the entrepreneur's dream. He quickly copyrighted and trademarked TSPMS to protect his idea and start fleshing out his model so he could show it to the world. He had been excited that this product would change his life—and the lives of others.

But the road had not been easy.

At first, he had some interest from his contacts, including human resource leaders, corporate executives, and small business owners. They knew him, trusted him, and liked what he had to offer. They were excited about TSPMS and how it would improve their employees' performance. After showing the product to these leaders, Johnny quickly got numerous orders and was excited to launch his software in multiple organizations around the country. Yet, just as quickly, this excitement faltered, as demand for TSPMS dried up.

The Golden Triangle
of Marketing

Johnny knew he needed to do something different, but he wasn't sure what. One of his mentors suggested Johnny speak to Mighty Mike, the city's number one marketing guru. Mighty Mike had helped numerous businesses be successful. His mentor said that Mighty Mike could help Johnny's company get to the next level.

Mighty Mike agreed to meet with Johnny for coffee to see if they were a fit to work together. Mighty Mike came in with an air of superiority; he had met hundreds of business owners and only chose to work with a few.

"I only work with those individuals who are willing to work for themselves. Does that describe you?"

"Of course," Johnny answered. "Do people ever say otherwise?"

"You would be surprised. What is your goal? Do you want to make a boatload of money, or do you want to help people?"

Johnny paused. No one had ever asked him what his goal was. He knew this question was necessary, but he hadn't given it too much thought. He wanted his product to be successful and reap the rewards, but he wasn't sure of his underlying motivation.

Mighty Mike jumped on Johnny's hesitation.

"You don't know," Mighty Mike said. "For the most part, your customers won't care why you are in business as long as the product works for them. However, if you don't know your reason for doing what you do, you will never be successful. When you hit a roadblock, you will need a reason to keep going. Money is never enough of a motivator to keep most people going."

Johnny smiled to himself as he walked towards his booth in the Market. Mighty Mike had been right. There had been many roadblocks to get Johnny to this Market—including technical issues, investor issues, marketing issues, and self-doubt.

1 Market: *What category of individuals would benefit most from your product?*

Narrow is best: Each product has a different market. It is up to you, the business owner, to understand who will be most likely to see the value in your product. Who has the problem that your product or service solves–and who has the resources to purchase it?

2 Message: *What words, visuals, sounds, tastes, etc., will intrigue your market to continue their journey to your door?*

A clear message that gets people to take action (i.e., Go to your website, pick up the phone, or buy your product).

3 Media: *What marketing tool will you use to reach your market?*

What mechanism will you use to reach your market? Social media, television or radio commercials, magazines, email, direct marketing, or one-on-one. You need to understand where your market is looking for a solution to their problem.

During their meeting, Mighty Mike had introduced The Golden Triangle of Marketing to Johnny. The Marketing Golden Triangle has three parts: Market, Message, and Media. Mighty Mike informed Johnny that to launch his product successfully, he needed to understand each of the three sides of the triangle. At the end of their meeting, Mighty Mike shared with Johnny this simple card he gave to his business clients to help them remember and follow the key points. (Coleman M. , n.d.)

Johnny had taken the card, disappointed that Mighty Mike had not chosen him to be a client, as she said he was too busy.

Initially, he had dismissed the postcard as just a silly handout, but as time passed, Johnny found himself relying on the information it shared. He used the principles to narrow his *market* and craft his *message* to better reach those who might purchase his product.

Johnny strolled over to where his team of five was setting up the booth. His messaging was now clear. He and his graphics consultant had worked hard not only to get people's attention—but to get them to take action. His favorite message they had created was, *"Let True Star Guide Your Employees' Performance."*

"How is it going?" Johnny asked his operations director, Sally.

"Good. We should have the booth ready for your inspection in about two hours."

"Perfect! I am going to walk around to see what the competition is like."

"I took a look around earlier. Our booth is one of the better ones. We've got this."

Johnny smiled and turned away. His stomach turned. He had bet not only his savings but also the jobs of his small, dedicated team on going to this Market. If it didn't work, not only would he be looking for work—but so would his employees.

Lessons Learned

Although Johnny was confident, he knew in the past he had made huge mistakes by believing what others had told him. In one case, he purchased an advertisement in a magazine distributed in golf courses in his service area. Before investing in the ad, Johnny had thought of Mighty Mike's wisdom. The magazine was the right place to reach his *market*—higher-level professionals—and he could craft the *message*. Johnny felt the magazine to be the perfect vehicle to get his product in front of the right people, so he invested money he didn't have. The salesperson guaranteed him it would help his sales.

Not one person showed any interest in his employee performance management system. Johnny later found that the person had scammed him. There was no magazine, no golf course, no sales potential.

A lesson learned, Johnny told himself, albeit a painful one.

As Johnny walked around the exhibition hall, he saw beautiful booths filled with pitch-perfect sales material. The vendors were all focused on getting the details right: talking to their staff, reviewing their verbal sales pitches, and making sure they had their "giveaways" set to draw the most attention.

"What do you think?" one vendor asked as Johnny passed. Johnny wasn't sure if the vendor was looking for positive reinforcement or constructive criticism.

"I know what you are selling and why I should buy it, so it's good."

"Thanks. First time here?"

"Yes. Does it show?"

"What about my giveaways? Do you think people will like them?" Johnny looked at the bright color stress balls, hand sanitizers, and travel masks.

"I guess. They relate to your product, health care."

"Thanks." The vendor turned away and started moving the stress balls around. Johnny had read all about the purpose of the "giveaway" in the Market's literature. They made people come up to your booth so you could start a conversation, and if you inscribed your logo on them, there was a chance they might call you as a result. But Johnny thought they were a waste of money. *In the world of the search engine, most people just google a vendor on their phones,* Johnny mused.

Johnny didn't like to waste money. Any money he spent needed to have a specific expected return. One of the "tricks" he had learned marketing his product was to give something of perceived value to a potential client—maybe advice, an article he had written, or a checklist he used. Offering such a resource always helped show his expertise and connect with the client. Most of his repeat customers continued to work with him, because he gave them additional content to support them—beyond the service he sold them.

Johnny returned to his booth and checked in with his staff. They were ready, and it looked like, even with the late start, the team would be done preparing the booth early. Johnny had promised them dinner, so he announced that he was going back to his hotel room and would meet them later at the restaurant.

On the way back to the hotel, Johnny connected with his social media manager to make sure that all current and potential clients knew he had a product at the Market. They had put together a special offer to encourage attendees to stop by their booth. Anyone who stopped by the booth during the Market would receive Johnny's white paper on employee performance.

One of the challenges Johnny faced early in his business was finding a customer relationship management system (CRM) that would benefit his company. The free ones didn't have the necessary functions his business needed, and others were highly expensive. He thought he had found one when a business contact introduced him to someone from a successful CRM company. It led to a terrible experience. After being introduced, Johnny decided to invest in his product. He also invested in making the product work for his business—adding customers and contact information, creating content to be used to reach potential clients. The product just didn't work as advertised. After struggling with the CRM for six months, John asked for a refund. The sales guy said it wasn't his responsibility, and he'd have to take it up with corporate. Corporate said it was the salesperson's responsibility to issue the refund. Johnny finally walked away, learning a valuable lesson: *not everything is as good as it seems.*

The First Day

It was the official first day of The Small Business International Market, and Johnny arrived early to help open his booth. A quiet hush filled the hall. Johnny knew in a few hours that potential customers would be streaming in, walking by his booth. He wondered if it all had been worth it.

Over the next ten days, thousands of organizational leaders and human resources professionals would evaluate the True Star Performance Management System and decide if he was worth the investment. He shook his head; he knew logically it was not *him* they would be evaluating, but on an emotional level, he couldn't help but think the rejection would be personal.

"Hi, Boss," Johnny turned to see Sally standing in front of their booth. "We are ready. People will love this product."

"I hope so."

"Never doubt."

They worked together doing last minute touches on the booth and making small chat with the vendors next to them. Johnny shook with anticipation; he hadn't been this nervous since he'd asked his wife to marry him. At least she'd said yes. He wasn't sure if people would say yes to his performance management system.

"Ladies and gentlemen, five minutes until the doors open," a speaker blared above him. Johnny took a series of deep breaths to calm himself—a simple technique he had learned back in his theater days.

"One minute," the speaker blared, causing Johnny to jump.

Sally, with her eternal optimism, smiled. "Here we go!"

"The doors are open. Good luck, ladies and gentlemen!"

The sound of thousands of voices filled the hall. Johnny watched as people walked by his booth. He knew some were there just to get the freebies, and others attended just to see what was new. A few lingered at his booth, reading the materials he had set out. Johnny waited until someone picked up his literature.

"Good morning!" Johnny greeted. "What interests you in a performance management system?"

The man looked up at Johnny groggily. He didn't say anything, just put the literature back down and walked away.

Sally shrugged.

"Tell me about your performance management system," a female voice said from behind Johnny. He turned to see a lady he guessed was a high-level human resources professional, either a director or chief people officer.

"What do you want to know?" As soon as Johnny asked this question, he knew he might have lost the customer. He hadn't listened. The lady had told him what she wanted to know.

"About the performance management system?" the woman asked again, more uncertainly.

Johnny gave his elevator speech about how he had come up with the idea and worked hard to show it at the Market. As he finished, she looked up at him and smiled.

"Thanks," she said—and walked away.

Johnny watched her stride further away, thinking it would be a long show if people just listened to his elevator speech and did not buy anything.

More people came. Johnny got lost in talking to them about his product and its purpose.

At the end of the day, sales did not meet Johnny's expectations. He made some money, but at this rate, not enough to cover his expenses or his employees' salaries. Johnny dismissed his team and walked back to his hotel room.

The Emotional Connection

Night had taken over the city. Not many people were on the street, dimly lit against the dark sky.

Johnny knew he was missing something, something big. He just didn't know what. *Why did that woman walk away? Why didn't my message ring true to her?* Johnny asked himself, thinking through the experience. He had told her the benefits and features, and still, she hadn't pulled out her credit card.

As he walked, he let his mind wander. His business coach had always taught him *the answer is in the question.* "You just have to find the right question," she had said. Johnny knew there was a reason why people purchased things. Usually, it was more profound than just the benefits and features of a product.

People will buy a product when they believe it will move them closer to who they want to be. For instance, Johnny thought, *I bought my home security system not because of all the features and benefits, but because it would make me feel safe. I had an emotional need for my family and myself to feel safe.*

The question then is, "What emotional need does my product fill for my customers?"

A smile crossed Johnny's face. Although his product's origin story was interesting, he realized that it was not a sufficient cause for someone to purchase his performance management system. He needed to determine what emotional need his product filled.

Johnny arose early and met with his team. He told them about his critical realization from the night before and asked them, "What emotional need does our product fill for our customers?"

He and his five team members discussed many options and finally decided their product represented *confidence* to their customers. They believed customers could say, "If I buy this product, I can be more confident that my team will perform well."

"So, what does that sound like in our sales pitch?" Sally asked.

"Actually, I heard it yesterday but had not realized it at the time," Johnny said. "In fact, I was annoyed when I heard it, since it went against what we were trying to do." Then he paused before asking, "Not that we were competing with each other here, but who in our group had the most sales yesterday? Sally pointed a finger at Julie, one of the sales representatives.

"I thought so," Johnny said. "Do you remember how you sold so much?"

Julie looked at Johnny, panic in her face. She shook her head.

"Because you were *you*. You didn't use the pitch we gave you. You told our potential customers how it had help *you*, how it had given *you* the confidence to do your work better."

Julie smiled and whispered to the sales representative next to her, "I thought I was going to be fired."

Johnny told his staff that he wanted them to share stories wherein a customer had achieved better results because the customer felt more confident. They discussed some stories from customers and also from the staff that could be used when talking to potential customers.

"Do you remember when the executive from XYZ Production Inc. called the other day?" Sally asked. "I think his name was Joel."

"Yes."

"He said that for the first time, he knew that his team was getting the guidance they needed to perform well. The True Star Performance Management System had given him the confidence he and his leadership team needed to manage their employees. They no longer had to guess at it. They knew what to do," Julie chimed in.

"Great. We can use that story. What other ones do we have?" Johnny asked.

They talked for a few more minutes, then shifted to the day at hand. Throughout the day, because the team focused on sharing stories with potential customers about how this product would boost their *confidence*, sales improved. The numbers were still below Johnny's expectations, but he was content with the results.

Johnny took his team out to dinner to celebrate their work. While eating, they honed their approach, each sharing the stories they had used and what they thought made them successful.

Johnny had always loved stories. Some of his best memories came from when his mom had read stories to him as a child. In college, he had studied theater and knew the power that stories held over an audience. In the corporate world, he had taught leaders to share micro-stories to help employees become more engaged in their work. Even a simple story about how they had overcome adversity helped employees stay more engaged.

Until today, Johnny hadn't thought about the importance of sharing stories to help sell his product. He had figured that if people saw the features and benefits, they would automatically buy what he offered. But sales didn't work that way. Customers needed to see for themselves. In the case of his product, this meant sharing stories so the customers could gain confidence.

The Struggle Is Real

The next day, sales continued to grow but still fell well below Johnny's original expectations. However, he felt that his team was doing well in delivering the message of confidence in their storytelling.

Still, something was missing in their selling technique—or possibly in his product, but he had a hard time thinking it was the latter. As the days went by and his team continued to struggle, Johnny got more anxious and worried that he would not make his company's payroll.

Johnny decided to walk around to see if maybe all vendors were having a problem selling their wares, and although this would not help his payroll, it would make him feel a little bit better. As he strolled by the booths, he saw some vendors doing well—and others doing no business at all. He assessed his company as right in the middle of the pack for sales per day.

The Small Business International Market had almost a thousand vendors. Johnny realized that if he wanted to stand out, he would need to do something unique. He saw the usual methods of luring people to products—long-legged ladies, hyperactive salesmen, giveaways, celebrities, and electronic bulletin boards. In a few cases, the gimmicks worked. Many times, they did not. Johnny's face scrunched as he tried to assess what was working.

"It's the product," a young lady said in Johnny's ear. "I'm Michelle. I work with the Market and help people with their sales."

"Hi. I'm Johnny. I have been watching these two vendors for about twenty minutes. From what I can tell, they have almost identical selling techniques. One is doing gangbusters, and the other is not."

"I told you. It's the product."

"Hype gets people's attention, but it doesn't sell. What sells are good products. I have worked here for over ten years, and those that are most successful have a good product."

"So let me ask: what is a good product?" Johnny asked.

"Good question, but you already know. A good product is one that fills a need, desire, or want in people's lives." Michelle looked at him. "Like your product."

"So, what can I do to get sales like that?" Johnny said, pointing at the vendor that had customers lined up at their booth like kids at Space Mountain.

Michelle smiled. Everyone wanted a quick win. "Their success won't last the whole show. Each third day, they do a special give-away to their clients. People show up, but then sales fall, and the salespeople are back hyping their product just like the other vendors."

"So, what should I do?"

"Learn how to make biscuits."

"Huh?"

"Do yourself a favor. Go across the street, and learn how to make biscuits. Ms. Bryde is one of my favorite success stories. She had a struggling business selling baking supplies. Now she runs one of the most profitable businesses in the city—and she happens to make the best biscuits. She has a biscuit-making class every morning. My suggestion if you want to sell more products: learn how to make biscuits." Michelle turned away, calling out to another vendor. Before she disappeared into the crowd, she turned around winked.

That wasn't helpful, Johnny thought as he walked back to his booth.

"Well?" Sally asked when he returned. "What did you learn on your walk-about?"

Johnny thought for a moment. He liked working with Sally. She had a great work ethic, but more crucial to Johnny was she thought like an owner, always finding ways the business could be better. As second in charge, Johnny relied on Sally to guide the staff, innovate new ideas, and keep him on task.

"Not much. What we already know: product first, and hype doesn't sell. And I have a lot to learn about selling our product in this Market. How is it going here?"

"Fine. The team is doing a good job, but I feel like we are missing something. We are leaving money on the table, but I am not sure why."

"Me too," Johnny said on a whim. "Do you like biscuits?"

"Who doesn't?"

"Meet me across the street at Mrs. Bryde's Baking Supplies at 8:00 a.m. tomorrow. We are going to learn how to make biscuits." Before he could think twice about what he'd suggested, he was committed.

Learning to Make Biscuits

The next morning, Johnny met Sally at Mrs. Bryde's Baking Supplies. The shop was tucked down an alleyway and not easy to find, but fifty other people were waiting to begin the cooking class when Johnny and Sally arrived.

The attendees took their seats at a large table. Each station held everything needed to make biscuits. In front of the room was a middle-aged woman, setting up while chatting with some participants.

"We will start in a few minutes," she cheerily said as she went about arranging her tools. She held no tension in her voice, no concern. She acted as if she were talking to friends in her kitchen.

"I'm not a baker," Ms. Bryde said from the front of the room. A hush followed. "And I haven't played one on television, although that is where my career started." She went on to explain how she'd developed a love of biscuits while creating a documentary on Southern baking. After it aired, people would ask her if she could teach them to make biscuits. And soon, she was offering biscuit classes.

As the morning progressed, she talked about what went into a good biscuit, the resources she found most helpful, and how with a little practice, the whole audience could make good biscuits.

Johnny was getting excited about actually making the biscuits. What a big surprise it would be for his wife if he made biscuits for her on Mother's Day! It seemed so easy!

"The key to good biscuits is the flour," Mrs. Byrd instructed. "If you live outside the South, you will have a hard time finding the right flour. I got so tired of getting unsatisfactory results that I created my own exclusive blend of flour."

Johnny and Sally took turns with the various steps. Johnny liked keeping his hands busy, so this was the perfect activity for him. Ms. Bryde walked around—encouraging everyone, making minor adjustments to participants' techniques, and telling stories of when she had failed. Johnny felt himself relax and settle into making the biscuits. Finally, their biscuits were ready to go in the oven.

"They look perfect," Ms. Bryde said as Johnny handed her the tray. She placed them into the oven.

"Can I buy some flour from you?" Sally asked.

"Of course, how much would you like?"

"Get two bags," Johnny heard himself say.

"Great."

"I was thinking of getting the sifter," the woman behind Johnny said. "Oh, and the rolling pin cloth—what did she call that? It will make cleanup so much easier."

As the class waited for the biscuits to come out of the ovens, participants walked around, looking at the products on the shelves. Most everyone had at least one or two items in their baskets.

Johnny quietly smiled to himself. *Michelle was right. I needed to learn to make biscuits.*

As they walked back to their booth carrying hot biscuits, a couple of bags of flour, and a set of biscuit cutters, Johnny knew what he had to do.

"Did you see what happened here?" he asked Sally.

"You made biscuits, probably the first thing you cooked since you were married?"

Johnny laughed in spite of himself.

"No. We just witnessed the best sales techniques ever."

"Meaning?"

"What percentage of people bought something from her?"

"I don't know for sure, probably at least seventy-five percent."

"Ninety percent. Only one couple walked out empty-handed. From the look of their biscuits, they have been baking biscuits since they were ten."

"Do you think people walked in there, thinking they needed to purchase a set of biscuit cutters?" Johnny said, holding up his biscuit cutters.

"No."

"Right! She made us *want* these biscuit cutters. She exposed a *desire* in us that we didn't know we had."

Sally's eyes lit up. "So, in a way, she gave us the *confidence* to make biscuits!"

Johnny smiled. He loved working with smart people.

On the way back to the Market, they discussed all the things Ms. Bryde had done to get people to purchase her products. "She was authentic. She didn't have a fancy culinary degree. She made biscuit making accessible for almost everyone."

Johnny thought back to the lady who had walked away on the first day of the seminar. She had walked out because Johnny had made it too technical. In this woman's mind, the process he was selling wasn't something she could do.

"Everyone in the class was prequalified to like biscuits and want to learn how to make them. She knew her audience. There were no cold leads, only warm, and she just needed to make them into hot leads."

"What I liked is that she demonstrated how to use everything before we started making the biscuits," Sally said. "I don't think I would've had the same confidence if she hadn't shown me how to use the products."

"How do you think we can do this with our performance management system?" As they arrived back at their booth, Johnny made a decision. "We need to shut down for the afternoon, so we can revamp our presentations."

"What? Can we afford to do that?"

"Can we not?"

Johnny called his team around him. He told them what he and

Sally had witnessed and how they would shut down and revamp their presentations.

The team members were in shock and hesitant, because sales had been going well. They were on target to have their biggest sales day yet.

"We will have our best sales day ever—*tomorrow*," Johnny confidently said. "We need to stop thinking about this as selling a product. We are selling confidence to our customers. They need to reach their goals." Johnny started scribbling on a whiteboard. "What was the last thing you purchased?" He turned and looked at his team expectantly.

"A drafting chair," a staff member chimed in.

"Why did you purchase it?"

"Because my other one was broken."

"Okay, so it solved a problem."

"Yes."

"When it worked, what did the drafting chair help you do?"

"Work at my desk?" the team member said hesitantly.

"Yes, and what work did you do at your desk?"

"Marketing brochures."

"Did you need that chair to make marketing brochures?"

"Yes...and I guess no. I could have used another workstation."

"So why the high table?"

The teammate smiled. "It made me feel important."

Everyone laughed.

Johnny smiled and wrote on the whiteboard: "It made you feel important."

"Yes! The stool isn't just *fixing* a problem for you. It is allowing you to be *confident* in your job. It gives you a sense of *importance*, which enables you to do your job well." Johnny paused. "Does everyone see the difference? We can sell the solution, or we can sell confidence. It is our choice, but people buy confidence more often than they buy a solution."

"So," another team member began, "how do we sell confidence?"

"I am glad you asked!" Johnny said with a smile. He turned to the whiteboard. "We follow the baker." He started to write. "First, we *understand* our buyers. As soon as we signed up for the biscuit making class, the baker knew we had a *desire* to make biscuits. She also knew from experience that she would have different levels of expertise in the class. Still, all attendees wanted to *improve* their biscuit making skills." He turned back to his team. "So, in what ways can we learn what our buyers want to achieve?"

"Ask them," Sally said. "I remember before she started the class, the baker walked around and talked to us."

"Great—what other ways?" Johnny asked.

For the next hour, they brainstormed ways they could better understand what their buyers wanted to achieve. They developed a list of *qualifying questions* to help draw out those goals.

"Once we know what they want to do, we want to offer them the confidence that they can make it happen. Tell me this: where does your confidence come from?"

"Knowledge!" a team member shouted out.

"Practice!" another said.

"People believing in me," yet another remarked.

"Having the right system in place. Knowing that I have the right information to take the next step," Sally said.

"Agreed. One of the things that amazed me was how confident I felt after the biscuit class. Mrs. Bryde gave us *confidence* by giving us the *knowledge* of how to make the biscuits—and a chance to *practice*. Now—in what ways can we impart that confidence to our potential buyers?"

They spent the next few minutes brainstorming ways to help their buyers gain confidence in using their performance management system and reaching their goals. What Johnny liked about his team is that they were open to sharing and listening to everyone's ideas. They soon had an extensive list of ideas. Johnny knew that they would need to minimize the list to a more manageable level.

"What made me comfortable purchasing products at the biscuit class," Sally began, "was our ability to use them.

"Me too."

"I was surprised by how much she gave away. I do not mean products. I mean recipes, her techniques, and of course, the free biscuits," Sally added. "Even if I didn't buy anything, I could still feel confident in making biscuits at home."

Johnny knew that this conversation was leaving out the teammates who had not attended, but he thought it was important enough to continue.

"Doesn't it build trust?" One of Johnny's teammates spoke up. "What I am saying is when I go to a business, and they offer me something with no strings attached, it builds trust."

"Yes!" Johnny then saw Michelle standing at the edge of his booth. He turned his head to face her. "Hi, Michelle."

"Do you like biscuits?" Michelle asked.

"I love biscuits," Johnny smiled.

"I heard you closed your booth down for the afternoon. I just wanted to make sure you were OK."

"Yes, just teaching my team how to make biscuits."

Michelle smiled and walked away. Johnny turned back to Sally.

"Can you take two of the sales reps and create a hands-on demonstration or class centered around our product that will give potential buyers confidence? I want to do a free ninety-minute class first thing in the morning every day for the rest of our time at the Market.

"Got it, boss." Sally smiled.

"I need a few volunteers to work with our social media manager to create social proof," Johnny added, moving on to the next agenda item.

"What is social proof?" a team member asked.

"Sorry—good question. Social proof is a theory that people will purchase items if they see other people purchasing those items. One study showed that people on airplanes were more likely to buy a snack if one of their row mates did."

"How would that work here?"

"Well," Johnny added, Holding a class will help us use this principle to our advantage, because we should get about 25 percent of those individuals in the class to buy something. Others will jump on the bandwagon, but I think we need to figure out other ways to use social proof to get our customers to buy."

"That is so true," the rep responded. "When I watch QVC, I am more likely to buy something if many other people are buying that item. I feel like I must be missing out on something."

"Yay! Great example. QVC is good at showing social proof. They also prompt a sense of urgency with their timers." Pointing to one of the sales reps, Johnny said, "Can you work with our social media manager to create *social proof* and a *sense of urgency* that we can use at the Market and on-line?"

"Sure—should I reach out to her?" the rep eagerly asked.

"Yes, start that conversation," Johnny instructed. "If she has any questions, have her reach out to me directly. Time is ticking. Let me know where you are with this process in three hours."

Johnny was feeling good. Not only was the team creating a better plan to sell their product, but also they were engaged in making it happen. In his mind, he was creating a plan to reward them with a bonus for their work—good sales or not.

Johnny assigned the rest of his team adjustments to make in order to optimize their setup for the rest of the Market. He wanted to make sure the booth could comfortably accommodate participants in a classroom setup. He left the team solving how to incorporate into the class some of the concepts they would typically discuss in their presentations with potential clients. Johnny wanted to catch up with Michelle and let her know about his class and make sure it was added to the Market's master schedule.

While talking to Sally, Johnny had decided to charge a small fee to attend the class. Johnny had discussed the idea of asking attendees to pay for a class with one of his mentors, Joel, numerous times. Both had done free training before. People always signed up but then didn't show up. Johnny knew it would be too easy for people not to show up if they didn't have a vested interest. Sally didn't like this idea initially, but Johnny convinced her that the value she and the team created would be worth the small entrance fee. After all, the biscuit class hadn't been free, and the room had been packed.

Seminar Time

Johnny was excited all night. He knew that he was taking the selling of his product to a new level. As he walked into the Market, he wondered to himself, *Will this work?*

His sales team had already set up for their first class. Instead of merely offering a product demonstration, Sally had created a class centered around improving an organization's performance. It just happened to center around Johnny's performance management system. During the lesson, the instructors (salespeople) would demonstrate how it created efficiencies within an organization.

"Good morning," Johnny said. He could see that Sally and her team hadn't slept much the previous night. He made a mental note that he would reward them after this was all over. "What do you need me to do?"

"Actually—nothing." Sally smiled.

"Really?"

"I got...actually, *we*—the team and I—got to thinking about how best to demonstrate the product's effectiveness. We decided that having someone who isn't an expert in performance management use it in real-time would be the best way to show how easy it is. So, Julie volunteered to do it."

Johnny raised his eyebrows.

"If that technique doesn't work in class today, we can change it for tomorrow," Sally said quickly.

Two dozen or so people had gathered in their extended booth. Johnny quickly calculated that if all had paid full price for the seminar, the cost of that day's booth rental would be covered, but nothing more.

"Welcome," Julie started. People quickly quieted. "We are so excited that you decided to join us today. Our goal in this class is to provide you with valuable information you can use to improve your employees' performance."

And get you to buy our product, Johnny thought.

"I want to get a sense of who is here today. Raise your hand if you have been in business for less than three years." Julie counted the hands. "How about less than five years? How about more than five years?" The remaining hands were counted. "Great. How many of you are lifelong learners—always looking for ways to improve?" Almost all the hands went up.

"I am too," Julie continued. "More accurately, I am now. When I started working with Johnny's company, I thought I knew everything I needed to be successful."

Everyone was intently listening. Julie went on to tell the audience about her first month on the job and all the mistakes she had made. The audience laughed. A connection began forming between Julie and the audience.

"At the end of the first month, my boss called me into her office to fire me." Julie looked over and smiled at Sally, her boss. "Or at least that is what I thought. As I waited for her to address me, I could feel the shame overwhelming me." Julie paused. "But she didn't fire me. She didn't even criticize me. Instead, she imparted a valuable lesson she had learned while working for Johnny."

Johnny realized he was on the edge of his seat as well. What lesson had Sally learned and passed on to her team?

"She told me to be curious. To ask questions rather than assuming I needed to possess all the answers. It was such a relief to know I could be open about what I didn't know. So, to pass that principle on to you, I'd like to request: in the next hour or so, please be curious."

The crowd was hooked. Engaged. Johnny could see it. The head nods, the quiet murmurs. Julie had connected with them and spoken right to the heart of employee performance.

"How many of you have experienced similar challenges with how your employees perform?" Julie asked the crowd.

Johnny took a deep breath. This was the moment of truth. If they hadn't done their job well planning this class, or if people didn't have similar challenges, Johnny knew the sales would be dismal.

Almost every hand was raised. Johnny sighed in relief.

"Tell me your story!" Julie gestured to an audience member. As they spoke, she listened, smiled, and commented where appropriate. She invited a few others to speak. The response was overwhelmingly positive and engaging.

"Great!" Julie said. "Here is what our team has done to overcome that challenge."

"They are all taking notes," Sally whispered in Johnny's ear, as they both watched Julie do her magic. "Now for the transition."

"What we realized," Julie said, "is that if we created a systematic approach that managers and supervisors could use, performance would improve."

Johnny quietly hoped that people would not leave, sensing that maybe a pitch was coming.

"Let me show you what we did." Julie pulled out the True Star Performance Management System Software and started demonstrating how it worked. No one left. She showed how easily their performance management system worked, its full range of operations, and the parts she liked the best. When she was finished, she asked, "Who would like to try it?" Almost all the hands came up. Julie randomly selected someone, allowing them to use the product while she kept talking. She had the audience's complete attention.

"We will allow everyone the opportunity to try it, and we can discuss individual implementation for your organization. But before we do that, I want to review the process we have used as an organization to increase our performance and achieve better business outcomes."

As the class ended, Johnny introduced himself to one of the partici-pants and asked how she liked the course. The woman raved about how helpful it was. In fact, she mentioned she was afraid that the product would sell out before she could purchase it and was glad when it hadn't. She ordered the enterprise solution for her 500-employee company.

Johnny inquired with a few more attendees, all of whom reacted as positively. They loved the information shared—and the actual opportunity to get hands-on with the product.

The vast majority of those who attended ended up buying Johnny's product. Although Johnny knew it was only the first class, he was filled with excitement for the possibility ahead.

"Please let your friends and coworkers know we will be doing this class for the rest of the Market," Johnny said to everyone. He searched for Sally to thank her.

"I don't think this is what you need," Johnny then overheard Sally saying to a customer. "Yes, it would help, but I don't think the cost-benefit analysis makes sense for your company."

Johnny blanched. Was she turning away clients? His face flushed with anger.

"Wait, here is our CEO—" Sally gestured towards him. "Let's see if we can find a solution that would work better for you." Johnny gave her a look. "Hi, Johnny. This customer has a small start-up and doesn't have the capital on hand to purchase our product. From what it sounds like, I don't think it makes sense for them to invest in it at this time. What other options might there be?"

Johnny smiled. "I love working with smart people," he said to Sally. "Let's see how we can solve your problem," Johnny added. He loved working with clients on the best way to increase performance in their business. He knew even a simple conversation could bring a future sale.

As the Market closed for the day, Johnny stood back and admired the dedication of his team.

"Best day ever," Sally said, standing next to Johnny. "We rocked at sales, and just as valuable, the team excelled at customer service. I am proud of them."

"I am proud of you. The demonstration you and the team created and executed was amazing. You learned how to make biscuits," Johnny smiled.

"Thanks for believing in me—in us," Sally responded.

"Where is our famous presenter?" Johnny asked.

"I let her leave early, since she had been up the whole night working on the presentation," Sally responded.

"We need to promote her."

"I thought you would say that. How about the position of the sales manager?" Sally had been thinking about this and was glad Johnny brought it up.

"Perfect. Let's tell her the good news at dinner tonight." Johnny turned to his team, bustling about the booth, preparing to end the workday. "Dinner is on me tonight. We had the best day ever, and we are going to do it again tomorrow."

Gratitude

At the end of the Market, Johnny's little product had excelled beyond his wildest dreams. For the first time since starting his entrepreneurial journey, he felt he was on the right path.

And it was all because he had learned to make biscuits. Before the Market closed for the season, Johnny went to thank Michelle.

"How did you know making biscuits would help my sales?"

"To be honest, I didn't. When I see someone who is authentic, prepared to take their sales to the next level, I send them to watch Mrs. Bryde. Some people get it. Some don't and think I am just a crazy lady."

"Crazy like a fox."

"Working with you and your team has been a pleasure. You deserve all the success you achieved at the market." Michelle started to walk away. "I will see you next year . . . at a bigger booth?"

"Yes." Johnny smiled. He realized that he had just been upsold, but he didn't mind. A genuine salesperson knows that the best way to get people to buy is to help them reach their goals. Mrs. Bryde knew this. Michelle knew this.

Now you, the reader, know it as well.

The Entrepreneur's Guide to Sales

Great, I Read Your Story, Now What?

I love stories. They allow us to share information, create empathy, communicate new worlds, and build bonds. As humans, we have used storytelling for a millennium. Before writing, all of our wisdom was shared through storytelling. The myths, legends, and lore of our ancestors were passed down from generation to generation this way.

We use stories to entertain. We use stories to teach others. We use stories to sell our ideas, products, and services. The story of Johnny teaches us the best practices of selling in action.

Remember, selling is asking someone to invest in you. Whether selling your idea, your product, or your service, someone must first invest in you. This investment ultimately might be of time, money, resources, reputation, or influence.

Although Johnny's story, as written, has many great lessons within it, I wanted to give you tangible actions you can take to improve your selling. The following section is designed to answer the question:

How do I sell?

It is a question I struggled with even though I had one of the best sales learning grounds while working at QVC, preparing our on-air talent. Numerous mistakes Johnny made, I also made. It was not until I started the entrepreneurial journey that I began focusing on how to sell myself, my services, my products, and my ideas. I was not initially good at sales. I had more fails than wins. But as time passed, I became better and better, reaching the point where I became the bestselling contract trainer for one of my clients in two categories I taught; for the rest of the categories, I was in the top five. My business started taking off, and I became a sought-after speaker, trainer, and workshop facilitator.

None of that would have been possible if I had not learned how to sell.

In the second section of the book, I will give you the necessary skills, techniques, and knowledge to achieve better sales based on the hard-earned lessons I learned on my journey and the research I discovered while working to be a better salesperson.

To successfully sell something, you will need to take the following six actions:

1 **Prepare to Sell: Do Your Research**

2 **Connect with Your Customer**

3 **Be Curious**

4 **Share Solutions**

5 **Close the Deal**

6 **Follow-up/through**

Let's dive in and explore how to implement these stages in your sales practice.

The Six Stages
of Sales Success

1 *Prepare to Sell: Do Your Research*

What Are You Selling?

It seems like a simple question. But it is not. In our fable, Johnny learned that he was not selling an employee performance management software system. He was selling confidence.

First, you must *define if you are selling a product, service, or idea*. When I started, I struggled to express what I was selling. Did I have a product, a service, or just fantastic ideas without market value? I remember talking to a prospect who asked, "What do you do?"

"I guide managers to improve their employees' performance."

"How do you do that?"

I balked at the question. I am sure I mumbled something semi-intelligent, but I did not have an answer. For my whole life, I had taught managers and employees how to improve their performance. Still, I had not clearly thought about how I would do that for this individual. Eventually, I created services I could sell, depending on the type and scope of help needed. I now offer interactive workshops, seminars, and leadership coaching to managers who want to take their performance management to the next level.

Also, consider *what problem your product, service, or idea solves*. In the upcoming section *Understanding Why People Buy*, I will discuss the primary motivations for why individuals will invest in your product, service, or idea. In most cases, they want you to solve an existing problem.

Next, you must understand *why your product is unique*—what we call in sales the *unique selling proposition* or the *unique value proposition*. This means you must research how other businesses solve the problem to pinpoint your differentiators.

For instance, let's say your problem is that you need to measure a wall. Stanley Tools has a tape measure to solve that problem. On the other hand, Apple solves that issue through a measurement app for iPhones. What would be the unique value proposition for the tape measure? How would Stanley Tool use a unique selling proposition to differentiate their tape measure from other options? What would be the unique value proposition for the app?

There is a brilliant book called *Why Should I Choose You? (in Seven Words or Less)* (Chamandy & Aber, 2015). In the book, Ian Chamandy and Ken Aber talk about the importance of understanding your business-specific promise—your unique value proposition. Their premise is that you need to define your business, product, service, or idea in as few words as possible to get people to take action.

What seven words describe what you are selling? Defining and limiting your explanation to a handful of words will significantly influence your impact in presenting. The goal is to understand the problem your product solves and its unique value proposition as it relates to your customers, so they can quickly see why it would benefit them.

Questions to Ask

- *Problem/Solution: What problem does my product, service, idea solve?*

- *What benefits and features does it give my customer, client, or boss?*

- *Unique Value Proposition: What makes my product, service, or idea unique? What differentiates it from my competition?*

- *Seven Words: What seven words would I use to sell my product, service, or idea?*

Who Are You Selling to?

Mighty Mike is a fictionalized account of an actual person I met named Mike Coleman (Coleman, 2020). I was introduced to Mike from a mutual business acquaintance. Our initial meeting went almost precisely as described in the story. However, unlike with Johnny, Mike did agree to continue working with me. Mike introduced me to the Golden Triangle of Marketing—the market, message, and medium. In our work together, he helped clarify the audience for my service. Like many new entrepreneurs, I had previously assumed that my service was so fantastic that everyone would want to invest in it.

That was not true.

Mike explained that some people would see value in my product. Some would have the problem the product solves, and others would have the resources to invest in my product. Only a tiny portion of customers would fit all three categories.

To succeed, you must narrow your focus to those individuals *who have the resources, see the value,* and *have the problem* your product, services, or idea solves.

In one of our first meetings, Mike worked with me to create an avatar of the person who would purchase my services. In sales, we use the term *avatar* to describe the ideal person in as much detail as possible to buy our product, service, or idea. In working with Mike, he wanted to know my customers' demographics, what they did for fun, where they spent their money, and what would hold them back from purchasing my services.

The more you know about your customers, the better you can focus your message on *them.*

At QVC where I worked, the marketing team did an unbelievable job of understanding who our customers were and what made them purchase items from us. They gave us words and images to reach our distinct audiences.

Of course, it is easy when you have twenty years of data, as QVC did. Starting out with any new venture, you must research and make your best prediction of who will purchase your product or service. If you are in a business setting and need to "sell" your idea to your boss, it still behooves you to research and understand who your boss is.

The goal is to understand your customer, client, or audience; why they would purchase your product; and what might hold them back from buying your product.

Reminder: the person purchasing your product, service, or idea may not be the one to use it. At QVC, we found a large percentage of buyers were female, although our product mix was designed to be used by both male and female buyers. Our research showed that female buyers were buying items for boyfriends, husbands, sons, etc. Similarly, in my business, I found that many of my buyers were from human resources; however, the end-users were executives and senior managers.

If your buyer is not the same as your end-user, you need to focus on why an individual purchases the product, service, or idea. Why are they investing in your product, service, or idea? What frustration are they trying to solve? In the case of QVC, many female buyers would buy gifts for their husbands—such as BBQ grills, sports apparel, or steaks—because they knew their husbands liked these activities.

Questions to Ask

- *What are the demographics of your ideal customer (age, gender, marital status, number of children, education, location, industry, buying power, etc.)?*

- *What goals are you helping them to reach?*

- *What frustration is causing them to look for a solution?*

- *What holds them back from purchasing?*

- *What influencers influence them?*

- *What magazines, podcasts, or social media outlets do they use?*

- *What conferences do they attend?*

- *Where do they spend their free time?*

- *Who is a good avatar (visual representation) of your customer?*

How Are You Selling? What Medium Are You Using to Reach Your Audience?

In television retailing, we used airwaves to sell our products. In contrast, one of my current clients is a direct marketing company and spends most of its marketing budget on sending flyers to potential customers. As an entrepreneur, I use networking and social media.

Your objective should be to build awareness about the problem that your idea, service, or product solves and get the audience to see the value of investing with you.

For your marketing to be effective, you also need to understand where your customer is reachable. For instance, when trying to get retailers to purchase your product, social media is probably not your best avenue. In contrast, a conference where retail buyers regularly attend would be a good bet. Before our story began, Johnny spent a lot of time deciding on the right market for his product. You must do the same. Decide how and where to reach your customers or clients. Revisiting who your customers are will help with this step.

Questions to Ask

- *Where do your customers spend their time?*

- *What influencers influence their thinking?*

- *What magazines, podcasts, or social media outlets do they use?*

- *What conferences do they attend?*

2 Connecting with Your Customer

Defining Your Message

One of my life lessons has been realizing that we all see the world from a different vantage point, which is derived from our experience, education, and environment. The blend of those components forms how we see the world.

When we communicate, we naturally tend to try to connect from our own perspective. The best way to think about this is that everyone has a language they use to communicate. If we aren't speaking someone else's language, they will not be able to understand us. This disconnect becomes critical when trying to influence someone to invest in our product, service, or idea. We must learn—and use—their language.

Our message is not just the words we use, but also the imagery. In marketing, the stories are displayed through copywriting and design. Large companies spend millions of dollars to create the perfect mixture of words and images that influence us to invest in their products, service, or ideas. Entrepreneurs often work with a professional team to hone a message to reach their customers. Here are a few tips for those of us bootstrapping an entrepreneurial idea, even without a big budget or team:

Use their language
Understanding your customers will help you use the words and images best suited to them. For example, when I am selling to a hard-nosed executive, I would focus my messaging

on profits, earnings, and goals. In contrast, if I am selling to a stay-at-home mom, I would focus on love, tranquility, and family.

Each industry has its own language as well. When I first started working in manufacturing, many terms were new to me, like agile and benchmarking. As you approach a client or customer, you need to use phrases and words that fit within their world. If you do not, you will need to spend more time explaining words and phrases to that individual, hindering smooth communication.

Create an emotional connection

People buy based on how a purchase makes them feel. If you can create an emotional pull for the buyer, they are more willing to buy your product, service, or idea. Even in the example with the hard-nosed executive, you can tap into his sense of pride in his ability to negotiate a deal. Or in the story of the Market, Johnny realizes he is selling confidence to his potential clients. When you watch television, advertisers work hard to solicit an emotional reaction. They know you will remember that emotion long after the product's details have faded away. In the upcoming section, *Understanding Why People Buy*, I will discuss the two fundamental emotions that cause most people to purchase.

Ask them to take action. In the copywriting business, this is called the "call to action." The call to action doesn't necessarily have to be to invest in your idea, service, or products. Many organizations use their copywriting as a way to start a conversation. They will end with "call us for more information" or "click here to get a free download." We can also achieve this in person by building the conversation to ask a customer to take action.

For instance, when I am in a conversation with a potential

client, I may ask something like, "How would improving your employees' performance benefit your organization?"

The response I hear most often is, "If I could get my employees to perform better, we would have better sales, a better work environment, and less overall grief."

"What is the value of better sales?"

"Immeasurable."

"Great. Let's start working together, so you can deliver that for your organization. Here is what I want you to do. Tomorrow, I will send you my proposal. Sign it and get it back to me, and we can schedule a time to start working together."

The difference in delivery

Your message will vary depending on how it is delivered to your customer. What you say *in person* will be different than what you convey *in an email*, which will be different than what you *write on your direct marketing pamphlet*.

Questions to Ask

- *What language does your potential client or customer speak?*

- *What industry language do they speak?*

- *What is their life perspective?*

- *What words might open them to new possibilities?*

- *What emotion are you trying to elicit when using your product or service?*

- *Which of your words or acronyms might confuse them?*

3 *Relatable: The Hidden Power of Influence*

People buy from people they like. This old adage has influenced millions of salespeople throughout centuries, because it is true. Think about it.

Who do we like? People we trust.

I was once in a seminar where the facilitator asked if we trust people automatically, or if they have to earn our trust. Unsurprisingly, people fell on both sides of the argument. However, if you asked people if they trust salespeople, I am sure you would get a resounding *no*. At one point or another, we have all have been taken advantage of by an unreputable salesperson.

So, even before we begin selling, we have a barrier to creating a sale.

What if, instead of trying to "sell" someone, we built a mutual relationship focused on helping them reach their goal or objective? In doing so, we would build trust. Building a relationship doesn't have to be a lengthy process. Even the small act of asking someone about themselves can start fostering a connection. If you use curious follow-up questions to learn more, people will begin to trust you.

A simple technique is to use open-ended questions—questions that don't garner a simple answer, like yes or no. For example, in a sales conversation, a question you can ask is, "What is keeping you up at night?" or "What challenges are you dealing with right now?" After they respond, you can express sympathy and concern. In our Market story, when Julie is starting the workshop, she asks the individuals to share their challenges around employee performance. She then quickly expresses sympathy for them and asks follow-up questions like, "What have you tried to do to fix it?"

The book *Principles of Marketing* from the University of Minnesota (University of Minnesota, 2010) describes the four different sales relationships: transactional, functional, affiliative, and strategic.

Transactional
In sales, a transactional relationship is usually centered on a product that a person can buy with little or no interaction with a salesperson. For instance, purchasing something at a big box store is a transactional purchase.

Functional
A functional relationship develops due to the routine or habit of the purchaser. If you regularly go to your local grocery store, you will develop a functional relationship with the associates. They may know that you like to purchase fish on Thursdays, for example.

Affiliative
An affiliative relationship develops when a buyer needs the knowledge or ability of the seller. If you plan to purchase a house, your relationship with your realtor will be affiliative. This may show up in the corporate world when you ask a higher-up to invest in your idea.

Strategic
Strategic relationships are developed to create a win-win where both parties benefit from the connection. Both will usually invest money and time into the relationship to increase overall value. An example is the Ford Motor Company, wherein Goodyear supplies them with tires. Both the tire company and the car manufacturer benefit from the relationship, since the better the tires are, the better the car will perform.

Trust is a component of each of these relationships; however, trust is most crucial in affiliative and strategic alliances due to their higher risk level. If you don't get the right product, or the rapport sours with the transactional relationship, very little is lost. However, if a strategic relationship fails due to damaged trust, both sides potentially lose significantly.

So, how does a salesperson build trust?

Building trust is about doing what we say.

Follow Through on Your Obligations. When I talk about trust, most people will say, "I trust people when they do what they say they will do." Even in the small stuff. If you said you would follow up with a phone call and don't, people start doubting your sincerity. If you cannot keep a promise, don't make it.

Be Relatable. I don't mean to add phony smiles and insincere compliments. A straightforward way to relate to others is to ask questions about them. Doing so gives you insights into the person and their challenges. Also, be vulnerable. Open up. Tell them why you believe in this idea, product, or service. Don't just recite a script. Talk from the heart.

Be an Active Listener. Active listening requires not holding to an agenda. Focus on how your customer expresses their concerns. Respond with statements and questions to clarify the concerns your client articulates. A weak salesperson listens only to move their agenda along, trying to convince a client to buy before finding out what their interests are. In this book's skill-building section, I will detail how you can build your ability to actively listen.

Be willing to say no. Tell potential customers what your solution can and can't do. At QVC, we built trust with our customers by directing our hosts and guests to tell customers if our products would not solve their problems. For example, in fashion, QVC does a good job describing how that particular item, dress, pants, and blouse fits different body types. One of our hosts was talking live to a customer about a product, and he recommended she not buy it. People were shocked, but it wasn't the right product for that individual. What this simple act did was reinforce that QVC was telling the truth on-air.

Questions to Ask

- *Do I come across trustworthy to my clients?*

- *How can I build trust with my clients and customers?*

- *What skills can I refine to improve at building trust?*

- *What type of relationship (transactional, functional, affiliative, or strategic) will best sell my product?*

- *What questions can I ask to build trust?*

4 *Be Curious*

Growing up, one of my favorite books was *Curious George* (Rey, 1941). It detailed the adventure of a curious monkey who was not afraid to try new things. Curiosity is defined as *the want or desire to learn something new*. To be successful in sales, you must be curious, asking questions to better understand your clients, customers, and audience.

Two ways that curiosity will help you are *qualifying your customers* and *better understanding the problem they need to solve*. At this point in the sales process, you should connect with people and work to understand if they are the right person to invest in your idea, product, or service.

Qualifying Your Customers

Hopefully, you took the exercise about defining your customer seriously. If not, go back and take a moment to determine who your ideal customer is. Once you have identified your ideal customer, you can now identify if the person in front of you is your perfect customer.

In sales, we call this qualifying the customer. Qualifying your customer starts by targeting those individuals within the demographics of your ideal customer. You "target" your ideal customer by marketing to them in the best medium to reach them. For instance, if you are looking for professional business people, you may use LinkedIn to contact them. If you are looking for sailors, you might use the magazine, *Sailing*. I do most of my targeting through networking or speaking at events where my prospective clients will be.

This is a good time to talk about cold calls. A *cold call* is a sales term for when you call, knock on the door, or message someone you think might be interested in your product but with whom you have had no previous contact. A portion of salespeople rely heavily on this method. If you've ever received a junk mail or a spam call or email, you have been on the other end of a cold call. For most products, services, and ideas, I don't recommend cold calls, because they involve a lot of effort for little return. The only exception I would make is if you cannot find anyone to make a warm introduction for you.

It's more productive to work with warm contacts, where you have been referred to an individual, or someone has reached out to you with interest in your product, service, or idea. The former is the more common method of acquiring a warm contact, where you are introduced by someone. Still, people will come to you if you have created a positive reputation in your market.

The second step in qualifying someone is to invite them to step through the door of interest. In the story, Mrs. Bryde uses her class as a qualifier for her products. She knows that people who purchase her products are interested in making biscuits. They have already stepped through the door of interest. This also happens in the selling of automobiles. When someone walks into the showroom, you can almost guarantee they are there because they are interested in purchasing a car.

A word of caution: in my networking circles, I see many individuals assume that because someone is open to meeting with them, they are interested in their product, service, or idea. In most cases, I find that all the other individual wants to do is sell their product, service, or idea.

Once you stand in front of your potential client, you should have a set of qualifying questions to identify whether they will become your ideal clients. In asking these questions, you will compare each potential client against the ideal customer you created at the beginning of section two.

If they aren't your ideal customer, you should walk away, leaving the door open for when they become your ideal customer.

Diagnose the Customer's Problem

Once you have decided that this person is an ideal client, you must help diagnose the challenge, problem, or issue you can help solve. In many cases, people will not be aware that the problem exists. Consider when Johnny and his operations manager left Mrs. Bryde's workshop. Both walked away with products to solve problems they were unaware they had.

Potential customers typically are more aware of the small frustration that keeps them from reaching their desired state. That nagging problem that, if fixed, would allow them to attain a higher level of performance.

Let's explore how leading questions help bring these needs to the forefront in the customer's mind. At the beginning of Mrs. Bryde's biscuit making class, she asks, "What happened the last time you tried to make biscuits?" Think about the possible answers to this question.

- *I never made biscuits.*

- *I had a problem (i.e., they were hard or fell apart).*

- *They were fantastic.*

For Mrs. Bryde, each of these answers gave clues to how she could help her client successfully make biscuits. With the last answer, Mrs. Bryde followed up with a simple, "Do you think you can make biscuits that good again?" With each response to her leading question, she was able to qualify the attendees in her class.

Leading questions are those that have your customer, your client, or your audience thinking about their frustrations in reaching their desired results. You can put your prospective customer into the mind frame of when their irritation was real enough for them to take action.

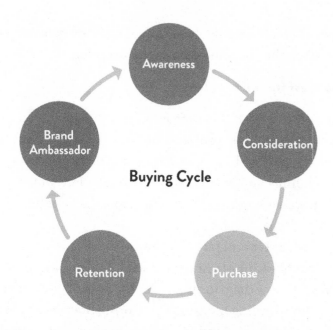

Leading questions also help you diagnose where clients are in the buying cycle. Are they aware of the problem? Are they considering possibilities to solve the problem? Have they made a purchase to try to solve this problem? Are they a brand ambassador for your company? The hardest person to sell to is someone who is not aware of the problem. This is one reason why cold calls rarely work. A customer you've cold called has no relationship with you or your product.

One powerful way to help an individual see the problem is to offer a free or inexpensive audit for them. This works well in the business setting and will get you in the door.

For instance, if you are a human resources consultant, you may let a prospect know that you will do a free audit of fifteen of the company's job descriptions. Or, if you are a dentist, you might offer to inspect someone's teeth for free. Or if your product cleans gutters, you might volunteer to show customers how well it works.

Reminder: everything you do as a salesperson should move your prospective client or customer to invest in you, your product, your service, or your idea.

Questions to Ask

- *Is this the right customer for me? Does this person fit my ideal client description?*

- *What problem, frustration, or pain do they have?*

- *What type of questions should I use to qualify this person?*

- *Am I willing to walk away if this isn't the right customer?*

- *If this person doesn't have the problem I fix, can I help in other ways? And can they help me with leads?*

- *Am I working with the decision-maker, or do I need a referral or to do more research?*

5 *Share Solutions*

Now that your potential customer is aware of the problem, frustration, or pain, you can offer the perfect solution. The customer will form a view of you that is influenced by how you present yourself. My friend, Toi Sweeney, is a renowned fashion stylist who works with executives and celebrities. She often reminds me that people will judge who you are and whether they can trust you in the first sixty seconds of meeting you. Your prospective client will evaluate you based on your appearance, approach, packaging, and introduction. This assessment happens automatically.

In public speaking classes, students are told that the audience will judge them in their first sentence. But that isn't correct. The audience starts assessing them as soon as the announcer introduces them, and their analysis of the speaker will continue throughout the presentation.

Your appearance should reflect your brand, industry, customer, and the occasion. You should show confidence, trust, and relatability to your customer. I did a presentation for a legal conference and made sure that I wore a suit. At QVC, we spent a lot of money and time making sure our hosts were dressed for their typical audience. Probably just as vital was that they felt confident in how they looked. It is incredible what a confident person can do.

In those first sixty seconds, your prospects ask themselves a variety of questions to assess whether you are trustworthy or not. As you move the conversation from problem to solution, you must show them that you have the right answers—and are the right person to deliver the solutions.

Presenting Your Solution

As a person who grew up in the theater, building and designing theatrical productions, my mentors always taught me to keep the audience in mind. In theater, the audience is the focus of the production. Our ongoing goal is to elicit an emotional response from them—maybe wonder, sadness, or perhaps anger.

When selling, we also must always keep our audience in mind. We should be speaking our customer's language. By language, I don't mean Spanish or French or Mandarin. Instead, use words and images that will connect with them.

For example, at QVC, when we sold kitchen items, our customers were home cooks and not professional chefs. So we focused on how the viewers could use the products to prepare food for their families.

One of the challenges in conversations is that we use words that mean different things to different people. For instance, when I conduct leadership seminars, I ask everyone to define *leadership*. Invariably, everyone has a different definition.

As a salesperson, you must carefully choose words and images to connect with your potential clients.

Personality Styles

Let's take a moment to talk about personality styles and how they impact potential clients' or customers' view of your presentations. There are many personality style assessments on the market—from DISC to Myers Briggs, Revised NEO Personality Inventory to The Birkman Method, and so on. The goal of these assessments is to help individuals better understand how they interact with others. They can also tell a lot about how people want to be communicated with or sold to.

Now, you can't go to every potential client and ask them to complete a personality assessment. However, understanding these assessments' basic principles can help you better understand your clients and how to communicate with them. As a note of caution, these assessments vary in their validations. They should be used only as benchmarks to start a conversation. You should adjust your questions and communication style to best fit the client in real-time, not on a prescribed personality block.

Most two-factor assessment models use a gradation based on the responses to the questions. In one model I used, there were two fundamental questions.

1. *How comfortable are you with showing your emotions?*
   (i.e., Are you "reserved" or "comfortable" when sharing your feelings? Do you emote, or do you control your emotions?)

2. *How comfortable are you with expressing your point of view?*
   (i.e., Are you more of the "telling" type or the "asking" type? Are you direct or indirect when trying to get your point of view across?)

When using these questions to understand customers, you can better ensure you tailor your delivery so they can best hear you. Take someone who is reserved and curious, for example. You will need to present them with facts and figures. Yet, with someone who is more telling and emotional, you can share stories that exemplify the product in use.

Another aspect of presenting your solution is knowing your product, service, or idea well enough that you can answer almost any question. Pharmaceutical reps must fully understand their products, benefits, side effects, what studies have been done, etc. To gain this knowledge, they study to learn, memorize, and prepare answers for any and all questions a doctor might have. You need to do the same. In some cases, your product or service is a result of developing, creating, or experiencing a eureka moment on your own. In other cases, you are selling another person's product, service, and idea. Either way, you need to understand how your solution will benefit the consumer.

At QVC, our hosts were geniuses about learning their products. They would study, meet with our internal product buyers, or talk to the vendors. In many cases, they would use the product themselves, so they could understand the experience from the consumer's point of view. They went through this background work to become fully informed.

This doesn't mean you need to be THE EXPERT on the product. You just need to show that you know more than your prospective client does. Grant Baldwin of The Speakers' Lab, a speaker's classroom, tells a great story about going to his mechanic to fix his car. He knew that his mechanic wasn't the best in the whole world, but the mechanic knew a lot more about cars then Grant did.

You should always know more about your product, service, and idea than your customers.

So, how do you engage a potential client in the solution conversation?

Start by being curious and asking questions about their issues, frustrations, and pains. Then ask, "What have you done in the past to deal with these issues? How did that work for you?"

The goal is to position them to start considering other possible solutions. Once they enter this mindset, it is time for you to present your solution.

Questions to Ask

- *How do you show up? How do people see you?*

- *What "language" do you need to speak to reach your customer?*

- *What personality style is your customer?*

- *What steps must you take to move your customer or client from awareness to consideration?*

- *Can you communicate the benefits and features of your product?*

Demonstrating the Product, Service, or Idea Value

Your customer or client will know the value of your product, service, or idea as soon as they start to use it (or not). Yet the challenge for you is: how do you show the value of your product, service, or idea?

Purchasing Value Risk. Before I show you ways to demonstrate the value of your product, service, or idea, let's talk about *Purchasing Value Risk* (PVR). PVR is the level of risk an individual must assume to invest in your product, service, or idea. For example, buying a candy bar in the grocery checkout line has minimal Purchasing Value Risk, whereas buying a new car has a lot.

What is the Purchasing Value Risk for your product, service, or idea?

As a salesperson, your goal is to reduce the risk for the person you ask to invest in your product, service, or idea. Some companies will provide a thirty-day guarantee to minimize the Purchasing Value Risk. Many used car companies are now granting a full refund if you bring the car back within seven days, no questions asked.

What will you do to reduce your customers' Purchasing Value Risk?

Part of overcoming objections about Purchasing Value Risk involves demonstrating the value of your product before the purchase. The bigger the perceived value compared to the price, the more willing the consumer will be to take a risk. You demonstrate value through expertise, social proof, giving value away, and displaying the product with the consumer.

Social Proof. Consumers' behaviors are influenced by what others do. In the Market story, Johnny references a study done on passengers on airplanes. In 2012, Professor Pedro Gardete of Stanford University examined the impact of individuals' buying habits in an aircraft's same row. What he found was astonishing. Passengers were 30 percent more likely to purchase something if one of their row mates bought something. He then looked at passengers traveling together. They purchased even more if someone else in the row bought something (Gardete, 2015).

The bottom line here is that people will purchase items if they know other people are buying them. Their desire increases for what that product, service, or idea can give to them. Large and small brands use this technique by asking or hiring social influencers to talk, chat, snap about their products.

QVC uses social proof as a way to influence people to purchase their products. They do this by sharing testimonial phone calls where the customer calls to tell the program host how much they love the product. They also do this by showing how many people have purchased the product during the on-air sale.

Mrs. Bryde used social proof during her classes. As she rang up a sale, she used more prominent gestures to draw attention to her buyers' behaviors. She spoke directly to the buyer and said, "You will *love* this product." In doing so, she signaled to everyone else in the room that someone was buying a product, and it was OK for others to do the same.

I used this technique when I worked in the corporate world. When I had an idea that I thought my team or my boss would be resistant to, I would get a magazine article or an example where another organization or department had done it. This technique at least opened minds to the possibilities.

Reciprocity (Giving Someone Value). In his groundbreaking book, *Influence: The Psychology of Persuasion*, psychologist Robert B. Cialdini discusses the six levers of influence (Cialdini, 2006). One of those was reciprocity. He defined reciprocity as the theory that people are more likely to treat others in the same way others treat them. This means that people are more likely to invest with you if you have already given them something of perceived value.

Even a simple piece of candy can change someone's behavior. A group of researchers experimented with how diners tipped based on whether they received a piece of candy with the check. In the first experiment, they compared the differences between diners who received a candy piece and those who did not. What they found is that tips increased by 14 percent. The second experiment compared the difference between diners who received a single piece of candy and those who received two candy pieces, given at different times. In the second experiment, tips went up 23 percent (Strohmetz, 2002).

In both cases, the most significant difference was the simple act of asking the diners if they would like one mint or two. This act allowed the customer to focus on the value of the exchange.

So, how do you give a potential customer or client value without giving away the store? First, determine their challenge and what they could perceive as valuable. Then provide a low-cost, high-value solution. When I am speaking, I usually give away a free chapter from my book. If I am trying to win coaching clients, I might offer them a complimentary coaching conversation or free assessment. The key is to provide them enough information to experience the value and want more. As we say in show business, always leave them wanting more.

The value is always in the eye of the perceiver. Both Mrs. Bryde and Johnny used the perceived value of their workshops to create a sense of reciprocity. Using similar techniques in my workshops, I ask the participants how much value they received from the seminar. This opens the conversation for more workshops, meetings, etc.

This technique also works with products. At QVC, we would offer what we called a *gift with purchase*. If you purchased one of our products, you'd receive an additional reward. You could also do this ahead of a sale by offering an article to help your customer solve a small aspect of their problem.

Demonstrating the Product. One of the keys to QVC's success is showing the product to their customers. For a moment, visualize yourself walking into a store to purchase an air fryer. You read on the package that it will save you time in the kitchen. You also learn that it's ideal for family meals and will reduce fat by 88 percent. If you are in the market for an air fryer, that might be enough for you to purchase it.

Now, visualize yourself watching QVC. The host places frozen French fries into the air fryer and starts talking about the benefits of not using oil to fry your food, including reducing 88 percent of the fat you eat. Once the French fries are cooked, the host pulls the fries from the unit and tastes them, exclaiming how delicious they are. Suddenly, you are craving French fries and pick up the phone to order.

QVC knows that if you see a demonstration, you are more likely to buy the product. Could you imagine buying a car without taking it for a test drive? The more we understand what the product can do, the more likely we are to purchase it.

Not every product, service, or idea is easily demonstrated for every customer; however, there are ways to create a demonstration in the mind's eye of our customer, client, or boss. I asked you to visualize a presentation of an air fryer on QVC. You pictured the uncooked French fries going into the unit, and you pictured them completely crisp coming out of the unit. Your imaginings might have even made you a little hungry. This is the power of storytelling.

How can you demonstrate the value of your product, service, or idea? You might have to use data to help the person create a perceived value in their mind. If you are selling a snowplow attachment in the summer, you can't demonstrate how it works, but you can create an image of the customer's product:

Did you know it takes the average person two hours and thirty-three minutes to shovel their driveway? But with this attachment, from start to finish, including the plow's installation, the average driveway can be cleared in less than forty minutes. That will save you an hour and fifty-three minutes.

In fact, I have a video showing my mother plowing her driveway. Let me show you.

Johnny and Mrs. Bryde demonstrated the product they wanted people to purchase in their workshops, while creating value, building relationships, and showing social proof.

Questions to Ask

- What social proof can I use to show the benefits of my product, service, or idea? (Think testimonials, reviews, or influencers.)

- What steps can I take to reduce the Purchasing Value Risk to my customer? Can I offer a guarantee or warranty?

- What value can I provide to my potential customers or clients at a low – or no-cost solution?

- How can I best demonstrate the value of my product to potential users?

6 *Close the Deal*

It seems a simple enough activity: ask your customer, client, or boss to invest in your product, service, or idea. But, more often than not, this step doesn't happen. Why? Because we expect that showing the customer, client, or boss the perfect solution will be enough to elicit an immediate desired action. But that's not typically how it works. We have to go one step further. Nothing will happen unless we make the ask.

The other day, I facilitated a workshop and upselling of an advanced workshop for the attendees to invest in. Throughout the day, I talked about why this advanced class would help them reach their goals, discussed its benefits, and showed them testimonials from past attendees. But no one it was buying it. Then I realized—I hadn't asked them to buy it. So I stopped in mid-sentence and said, "I want to take a moment and give everyone the chance to sign up for the advanced class. If you do it today, I will give you an in-seminar discount."

Fifteen percent of the class signed up on the spot. If I hadn't asked, the percentage would have been closer to 5 percent.

Ask Them to Take Action

Selling is asking people to take action. Remember, I defined selling as influencing a customer, client, or boss to invest in your product, service, or idea. Depending on the investment, the action will be different. It may be having them purchase your product. It might be investing their relationship capital in moving your idea forward. It might be spending their time to attend one of your workshops.

The sales process is all about moving a potential client or customer through the various stages to the point where they are ready to invest. At the start of the sales process, you should be very clear about what your goal is. How will you make your customer, client, or boss take action?

At QVC, our host would recite our phone number repeatedly throughout the sale, so our viewers were reminded how to take action and get the product. In my workshops, I hand out a form near the end of the class and ask them to fill it out with me. For you, it might be as simple as pulling out your credit card machine and having them complete the transaction right there.

Skill Building

The Pitfalls All Entrepreneurs
Need to Avoid

Barriers to Buying

By this point in the sales process, you have the client or customer ready to take action. They see the wisdom in investing in your product, service, or idea. Yet occasionally there are still barriers to investing. It is your responsibility to remove those barriers.

Let's look at a few of the barriers that might get in the way.

I am not the decision-maker. At the end of the sales process, prospective customers or clients will tell you they aren't the ones to make the final decisions; all they can do is make a recommendation. When this happens, it is very frustrating, because you spent time moving the person through the sales process to find out they were not the decision-maker. This challenge is your fault. You simply failed to ask the qualifying question: are you the decision-maker?

If this happens, build on this person's excitement to inspire them to take action. Ask, "Can we talk to the decision-maker now?" and follow up with, "What resistance do you think they will have to making the purchase?"

Sometimes the decision-maker is not the authority figure. When working in the corporate world, I discovered that the first person I needed to invest in my idea was often the executive assistant. They were the gatekeeper to the boss. If I could get them invested in my vision, I would get better access to the executive. They would also be a champion for the project or idea, making the executive more likely to invest.

It costs too much. This barrier isn't actually about money. It is about value and trust. The client is looking at the potential return on the investment and not feeling comfortable with the risk level. Either you haven't done an excellent job showing them the value of the product, service, or idea, or you haven't spent enough time building up trust.

Go back and revisit the *value for the customer*. Ask, "How valuable would it be if we fixed this problem for you?"

We are looking at other options. Early in the sales process, ask what alternatives they are reviewing to solve their problems. Do not be afraid of competition. Competition can show why your product, service, or idea is a better solution. Use this information to do your research and provide a more affordable comparison. This builds trust and also provides the client with value.

Confusion. Your customer or client may not come out and say, "I am confused." Either you gave them too much information, spent hours going over the benefits and features, or are not clear on their problem. Often, as we've explored, when you talk to a client or customer and discuss challenges, you will bring up questions, issues, or concerns that they didn't realize they needed to address.

Barriers are just part of the sales process. The more you sell your idea, product, or service, the more prepared you will be to overcome obstacles earlier in the sales process.

Questions to Ask

- *What tools will you use to overcome barriers?*

- *What questions will you ask to see if the person you are talking with is the decision-maker?*

- *Review your proposal. Is it simple enough to inspire an easy decision?*

- *Who are your competitors? How does your product differ from theirs? Why is yours better?*

- *Personally, how will you handle getting a no? How will you push yourself to keep moving forward?*

Create Urgency

How many times have you heard a customer, client, or boss say, "I need to think about it"? Ugh! People like to say they need to weigh all the options. Discuss it with their spouse. Review the budget. What they are actually saying is, "I don't see the urgency in purchasing your solution right now."

It is your responsibility to create urgency with a customer.

I got my car serviced the other day, and the dealership found a nail in my tire. Because of where it was located, they said they would have to replace the tire. Do you think I had them replace the tire?

I didn't.

Why? Because the service agent did not create any urgency. She didn't tell me that there was a significant risk of driving on this tire. She didn't tell me that she could give me a loyalty discount. She said they could replace the tire, but it would be best to replace all four tires—*cha-ching*! Also, if I wanted to replace the one, I would have to sign a waiver.

Urgency can be created in four ways.

The first is by showing the customer, client, or boss the risk of waiting. *If you wait, there could soon be catastrophic damage.* Let's say you're a plumber, and you find a small leak in a person's hot water heater. Could you paint a picture of what could happen over time? Or maybe you sell HR solutions. Could you paint a picture of the consequences of waiting? Perhaps if the solution is not instituted, the Department of Labor will come a-knocking?

Urgency is created when the risk of inaction is not an option. Your customer, client, or boss must do something to solve this problem, or the consequences will negatively impact them.

The second way to create urgency is around the offer. At QVC, we generated need by using a simple timer on the television screen. "This offer will end in three minutes, two minutes, one minute." If you've ever purchased a car, you've heard the salesperson say, "This offer is only good until the end of the day. If you don't purchase it now, I will have to put your vehicle back on the lot."

A third way you create urgency with the offer is by adding value to it. For instance, as I've shared, in my seminars, I have said, "If you purchase a membership today, I will give you this informational package for free." This doesn't mean that they could not get my membership some other time. It simply means that they would miss out on my informational package right then and there.

A fourth way to create urgency in the offer is by using seasonal pricing. I do this when I know people are less likely to invest based on the time of year. For example, in August, people are less likely to invest in a workshop, so I might offer a discount for bookings during that month.

Questions to Ask

- *What action do I want from my customer? What would their investment be?*

- *How will I create urgency when talking to my customer, client, or boss?*

- *What barriers might customers or clients have around my product, service, or idea, and how can I overcome them?*

- *When in the sales process, do I stop and ask potential customers or clients to invest in my product, service, or idea? If not, how can I make sure I am working this step into my process?*

The Follow-Up

After the sale, following up is critical to creating a lasting relationship with your customer. Lasting relationships are essential for the long-term health of your business. If I purchase your product and am happy with it, I likely will buy another product from you. If I am unhappy, there is a good chance I will tell my circle of influence, and none of them will purchase from you either.

Follow-up can be as simple as sending an email—asking how the product is working and whether they have any ideas for making it better. It could be asking them to fill out a customer survey about the product or sales process. Or it could be keeping in touch through a newsletter, birthday card, etc.

I am astonished by how many vendors I have used over time, and none of them followed up. As an example, I had a vendor come service my HVAC system. I expected they would send me a reminder that it was time for my service again. They never did. So I ended up going with another vendor the next year.

The goal of the sales process is not to sell one item. It is to create a loyal fan who comes back time and time again.

Our realtor sends us an informational newsletter about house upkeep, market information, and our city trends. I usually skim through it before deleting it. She is offering value to me, at no cost, to keep her in the front of my mind if I need a real estate agent—or know someone who does.

Questions to Ask

- *What is the best mechanism to follow up with my clients?*

- *How do I create lasting value for my client?*

- *Can I create an ongoing service—or perhaps a membership program—with my product?*

Understanding Why
People Buy

In most sales workshops, books, and lectures, the instructor will say that people buy because they want to *avoid pain* or *gain pleasure*. On the simplest level, people buy something to change their situation, usually to improve their circumstances.

On a rational basis, this might be true. However, I believe, and research backs me up, that people typically purchase on an *emotional*— rather than *rational*—level.

The two most powerful emotions are *desire* and *fear*.

People buy because they **desire** a better future state of being or **fear** the status quo or a perceived future threat.

If you don't believe me, think about your last purchase. What was it? Why did you purchase it? For me, my most recent purchase was a glass cover for my iPhone. I was afraid that I would scratch my iPhone's screen. The purchase before that was a new grill. I had a desire to be a true grill master.

In accepting that desire and fear motivate people's purchasing habits, you can use these drivers to influence investment in your product, service, or idea. You create desire by using future-looking visualizations such as, "Picture yourself at the end of the day, a cool beverage in your hand, relaxing on your new deck." You ask clients to imagine what it would be like if they invested in the new deck.

You can create fear by using backward-looking visualizations such as, "Remember when you walked into your boss's office and didn't have the right answer? How did you feel at that moment?" In this case, you ask them to remember a time when they didn't have the solution they needed to be successful.

It is your responsibility as an entrepreneur, leader, and salesperson to pinpoint that desire.

When I worked as a contract trainer, I asked the people in the room why they were there. Most of them said to gain knowledge. At first, I used this to try and upsell them different types of knowledge, which would annoy them, because the training company had marketed my class as the place to gain a complete understanding of the subject.

For the first year, I struggled to move the needle on my sales. I watched other trainers and learned their techniques, but I couldn't seem to budge my sales. It wasn't until I asked myself, "What do my seminar attendees desire?"

The class was about compliance. So at first, I thought they desired protection—a way to reduce risk. I focused my presentation on showing the resources that would best offer protection. My sales did tick up, but I continued to struggle.

In the darkness of a back road in the middle of Texas, my epiphany came. They wanted more than *protection*. They desired *confidence*— in the decisions they were making at work. This realization changed how I taught and the products I offered for upsells. The changes worked! Over the next three months, I became the number one seller in two of my topics and ranged in the top three for my others.

Selling to emotion works, because you are not just selling a tactical solution. Instead, you sell them on the vision of their future better self, who they desire to be. In most cases, you connect with a profound emotional need within your customers.

As entrepreneurs, we also have desires and fears. Both desire and fear will impact how we interact with our customers. If we are entrepreneurs, we desire to achieve our own goals and reach a defined state of success. This can be both positive, helping us move forward, and it can be negative, because it drives us to spend all of our energy on our business. The other side of the coin, fear, pushes us away from situations that could benefit our company and ourselves.

When I first started my business, I was afraid to go talk to people about my idea. I hated networking. I hated selling. I hated marketing. There was a voice in my head that kept saying, "You can't do it. You shouldn't do it. People will laugh at you." I spent a lot of energy battling that voice until I put together a plan and started executing it. I started having success, my confidence improved, and the fear subsided. Occasionally to this day, fear will poke its head up and pull me back, but I take a deep breath, listen to the fear, and walk forward anyway.

Questions to Ask

- *What desires do your ideal customers, clients, or boss have?*

- *What fears do they have?*

- *How can you use this knowledge to create a better sales presentation?*

- *What are your desires? Fears?*

The Sales Abilities
All Entrepreneurs Need

Ability to Ask the Right Questions

My friend, Steve Van Valin, the CEO of Culturology (Valin, 2019), a consulting company that creates engaged organizational cultures, shared this concept to me while working together at QVC. He said, "To successfully find a solution, we must first know the right questions to ask."

In an interview with Bill Mohr, Dr. Jonas Salk, the polio vaccine developer, said, "...it (the solution) comes through asking the right questions because the answer preexists" (Salk, 1990). He went on to use the analogy of Michelangelo's statue of David. When Michelangelo was asked how he sculptured such an incredible icon, he said, "I saw him inside the stone, and I carved to set him free."

Asking the right question is an art—and essential in sales. As a salesperson, it is your responsibility to ask the questions to understand your customer—including their desires and fears. You must learn how your idea, product, and service can best serve that specific customer. Additionally, your questions can help filter people out and focus on individuals with a higher likelihood of investing.

The goal of questioning is to seek understanding.

In the sales process, you are trying to understand if the person is a potential investor (idea), client (service), or customer (product). In sales speak, this is called "qualifying the client." Are they qualified to be your investor, client, or customer?

- *Do they have the problem you are trying to solve?*

- *Do they have the resources needed to invest in your idea, service, or product?*

- *Do they have the resolve to invest in you?*

By asking these three questions, you will filter out individuals who would be less likely to invest in your idea, service, or product. Once you qualify your customers, ask questions to understand their situation. In his book, *Ask More*, Frank Sesno calls these "strategic questions"—those that focus on the big picture. As Sesno states in his book, *"[Strategic] questions sharpen the focus on the larger objective, the higher calling, and clarify what it will take to get there"* (Sesno, 2017). Here are examples of strategic questions:

- *What is your eventual goal? If you reached your ideal state, what would that look like? What are you trying to do?*

- *How will you achieve your goal? What steps have you taken to move closer to your ideal?*

- *What have you tried in the past? Why didn't it work?*

- *What would you be willing to let go of to achieve your ideal state?*

- *Have you looked at alternatives? What made you hesitant to go forward with another option?*

The other purpose of this type of questioning is it allows you to guide people down a path. People tend to get stuck in one mindset. They see the world from their past experiences. Questions can free them to see from another perspective. In *Ask More*, Sesno calls these "creative questions." In business coaching, we call them "curious questions." Either way, the goal here is to get the individual to rethink their framing and open them up to new possibilities. Here are some examples of such questions:

- *What if there were no limits? What if fear weren't an issue?*

- *Go big. What problem do you really want to solve? How would you solve it?*

- *Be CEO for the day. What would you do to change your company? Can you do that for your own life?*

- *What legacy will you leave?*

- *Congrats, you have succeeded. What decisions did you make to achieve your goal?*

- *Another way to guide people is to have them better diagnose their current state. Here are some questions you can ask to facilitate that process:*

- *What frustrates you about this situation? What emotion are you feeling?*

- *What barriers are holding you back from having a "frictionless" day?*

- *What causes you the most significant grief at work? At home? In life?*

- *If I could eliminate this challenge for you, what value would that add to your life?*

In my seminars, I ask participants, "Why have you invested your time to attend this class?" This is a strategic question to get participants thinking about their long-term goals. I am also guiding them to make a decision by asking them to value their learning—not only in terms of money but also time.

Exercises to Improve Your Technique

- Have a curious conversation with a child (ages five to nine). What type of questions did they ask you? Did you have the answers?

- Decide on one question, and ask it of ten people. What answers did you get? Were they the same? What did you learn?

- Work with your coworkers to create a list of qualifying questions.

Ability to Actively Listen

I will admit it. I am not a good listener. Because of my introvert tendencies, I am usually developing a response to a singular point, instead of taking the full conversation into account. Yet because listening is an integral part of what I do as a consultant, I have researched techniques to help me be a better listener.

Active listening requires being in the conversation—not just overhearing what the other person is saying. *Being in the conversation* means you participate in the discussion by asking questions for understanding, creating a safe place, encouraging different points of view, and focusing on full communication.

In *Crucial Conversations*, authors Kerry Patterson, Joseph Grenny, Ron McMillan, and Al Switzler state that before any crucial conversation can take place, we need to create a place where individuals can safely express their thoughts. If we react or quickly disagree, people will shut down (Patterson, Grenny, McMillian, & Switzler, 2012). I have seen this in many organizations where a hostile boss doesn't let his direct reports speak without criticizing their ideas. In time, no one says anything.

Instead of contradicting the speaker, ask a curious question to deepen your understanding of what the speaker expresses. Use either the simple phrase, "Tell me more about . . ." or "I am having a hard time understanding this point."

Another aspect of active listening is going beyond the words. As humans, we express ourselves using verbal and non-verbal cues. Just think of any teenager you know; I am sure they have perfected the eye roll. It says everything you need to know.

Non-verbal cues can include how a person holds themselves, facial expressions, the distance between the listener and the speaker, voice tone, and how someone dresses. We make judgments based on how we see others.

If you are indeed in a conversation, this means you are not only paying attention to what the person is saying but also how they are saying it. This ability to discern both what we hear and see takes practice, because in our society, we are taught to listen to words over non-verbal cues.

The other aspect of active listening is to be aware of the emotions, thoughts, and behaviors you are expressing. When I am in a safe environment, I know that my feelings are more likely to show on my face. When I am feeling unsafe, I have a good poker face.

A conversation's goal should be to find common ground and create a better understanding—even if you disagree with another's perspective. Encourage the other person to express their opinion, and listen in a non-judgmental way.

Active listening is a critical skill to develop as a salesperson, because it is used in all parts of the sales process. Use curious questions to qualify prospects, determine how you can best provide value, and help close the deal. Creating safety allows you to know your customers or clients better and help them achieve their goals.

Suppose you want to learn more about active listening skills. In that case, there is a helpful article in *The Harvard Business Review* called "What Great Listeners Actually Do" by Jack Zenger and Joseph Folkman (Zenger & Folkman, 2016).

Exercises to Improve Your Technique

- *Have a conversation with a friend. After it's over, write down what your friend said. Observe how they were feeling. Reflect on the outcome of your conversation. Then, write down how you felt and what you said. Ask your friend to read it and see if they had the same conversation.*

- At work, have a conversation with three or four people. Ask each to write down what they thought you discussed.

- Build curious questions that you can use to learn more about a subject.

Ability to Tell Stories

As I've shared, I love stories. Short Stories. Novels. Television shows. Movies. Graphic Novels. Video games. Plays. Stand-up comedy. Over the years, I have learned to appreciate a story for how it can move us and open our hearts to new ideas, people, and products.

What is a story?

Humans have been telling stories for ages. Before the advent of writing, stories held the culture, myths, and legends—and were passed down from one generation to the next. Stories guided people on how to behave, where the best food was located, and how to explain the unexplainable.

A story is the sharing of an event or series of events, either actual or fictitious. Since we were babies, we have been learning from our families' stories about life— stories they have learned from the generation before them. These stories, in turn, color the way we see the world.

When I was a young boy, my parents told me how my grandfather, Bill, who was an orphan, struggled to make it into college. Finally, with hard work and dedication, he got accepted into Bowdoin College. Even in this simple story, we can see the lesson: with hard work and commitment, you can be successful.

Stories are powerful vehicles for conveying ideas, concepts, thoughts, and direction. A good storyteller shares more than facts and figures. They color between the lines to give the reader a full experience.

The basic story structure includes setting the scene, introducing the complication, careening towards the climax, and finally finding the resolution. The setting of the scene gives your listener context for the story. The complication is the problem or challenge faced by the main character. The climax is the pivotal point where the problem comes to a head. The resolution is when the main character overcomes the problem or challenge, and the story wraps up.

Take a moment to compare your sales process with the short story structure. Do you see any similarities? What are they? As a salesperson, you are writing your own story. With your customer as the main character, you are their champion.

- *What is the environment your solution needs to take place?*

- *What is the problem or complication that needs to be solved?*

- *Who are the characters (customers or users of your product)?*

- *What or who is the villain?*

- *How will this story resolve itself?*

As part of the sales process, you can use stories to set the context, explain your product, and guide your customer to invest. When I am teaching new speakers, we spend a lot of time developing stories to help them get their points across. Suppose they are facilitating a class about active listening. In that case, I encourage them to share stories of times at work when they didn't listen to their coworkers. Through group activity, I help them ask audience members to share their stories. Doing so allows the concepts to stick.

Johnny's employee, Julie, used her story to convey how she benefited from Johnny's product. Mrs. Bryde also used her story about how she started making biscuits to illustrate how easy it is with the right products.

One of the myths of good storytelling is that stories need to be complicated or lengthy. Some of the most compelling stories are one sentence. Often attributed to Ernest Hemingway, one of the most potent examples is, "For Sale: Baby Shoes. Never Worn." In six words, the reader is taken on a short journey from optimism to sadness.

I refer to these as micro-stories and interweave them through my presentation to help set the context and guide the behaviors I want from my listeners.

Like this one: "As a salesperson, I always felt as if there wasn't a good manual on how to sell well."

If you're a salesperson, you will most likely agree with me in wishing there was an operating manual you could follow. I have just the book for you!

Good storytelling isn't just about the words. The process includes the non-verbal cues you use to sell the story. Your pace of words, hand gestures, clothing, and body movements can enhance your story.

The key to good storytelling is to practice your stories—deciding what you want to say, and when in the sales process you will say it. A great salesperson will tell a story that seems off the cuff, but it's not. Like an actor, they have practiced it so much that telling it becomes second nature.

Exercises to Improve Your Technique

- *Document a story for each part of the sales process that will move your customer or client forward.*

- *Practice telling your stories in front of a mirror, friends, or coworkers.*

- *Tell your story as part of the sales process. Ask yourself if it moves the client or customer forward.*

History is just the story written by the victor.

Ability to Influence Others

Besides delivering exceptional seminars, as a contract trainer, I am responsible for upselling products to attendees. When I first started, my boss strongly urged me to read the book, *Influence: The Psychology of Persuasion*, by Robert Cialdini. Based on Cialdini's research, he identified principles of influence that can be used to persuade other people to take action (such as, to help a customer invest in your idea, product, or service) (Cialdini, 2006). His book is a must-read for anyone wanting to influence others to take action.

As I read it, I was reminded of the years I'd worked in the QVC Talent Department with the on-air guests and hosts, teaching them how to sell on-air. QVC designed its on-air programs to persuade viewers to take action (i.e., buy products). Over the thirty-odd years QVC has been in business, they've developed selling practices that reflect the principles described in Cialdini's book.

Here are some tactics we used at QVC that you can use in selling your product, service, or idea:

Fear of Missing Out (FOMO). FOMO is a term used to describe the feeling of anxiety or envy associated with missing out. When I was growing up, we talked about it in terms of "keeping up with the Joneses." QVC fostered FOMO by creating scarcity with their products. We calculated that if the product at the top of the show sold out, people were more likely to purchase other products.

Social Proof or Consensus. Social proof is the impression that "if others are doing it, then it is OK for me to do this." One of my favorite stories on social proof's influence goes back to 1929, where the American Tobacco Company hires a group of women to smoke cigarettes while marching in the Easter Parade. They knew women watching the parade would want to imitate the ladies smoking cigarettes. It worked (Dworak-Peck, 2020). One of the reasons companies invest in influencers is that they know people who follow a particular influencer are more than likely to do what they do. We can see this with Kim Kardashian's influence on her social media fans.

Celebrity or Authority. People are influenced by those they see as authoritative. QVC plays to this by using their on-air hosts as experts and bringing in on-air guests with some type of credibility around the product: a technical expert in selling computers, a chef to sell cookware, a model to sell clothing.

Exclusivity. Exclusivity is in part about instilling FOMO, but it also involves creating desire before inclusion within the in-group— getting or achieving something not many other people can. QVC and other retailers often purchase products exclusive to them or buy the rights to specific products, so only QVC can sell these items in the United States. I learned this before my work with QVC. I went to purchase a specific brand name television, and I could only find the one I wanted at one particular retailer. As I researched, I realized that each brand would change small details, or in some cases, just change the item number so that the big-box retailer could say it was exclusive.

Create Belonging. People like to feel like they are members of a club or group. American Express used the influential slogan "Membership has its Privileges" to get consumers to use their cards and overcome annoyance that American Express couldn't be used everywhere. Almost all organizations play off the idea of belonging in some way or another. Airlines and hotels have memberships so you can accumulate their points. QVC and other retailers have members-only discounts. Many content producers use an exclusive email or social media group to create a sense of belonging. They then use it to upsell products, services, or ideas that their clients might want.

Social influence is about persuading others through social proof and social cues. In the Market story, Johnny talks about how social proof will get more people to purchase his product. We also discussed social proof in the "Hidden Power of Influence" section of this book.

QVC was an excellent teacher of these principles, and over my years there, most of their ideas became ingrained in me. As I started as an entrepreneur, I began to see these principles in action outside of QVC. It made me smile to hear others use the techniques that had been so important to QVC's success.

Give Away Something to Get Something. What Cialdini calls reciprocity is an understanding that people are likely to treat others in the same way others treat them. If you give someone something of value, they are more likely to look at you in a good light. You will see attempts to use this technique at conferences when a company offers something to attract people to their booth. Influence is about trust. Suppose you give something of perceived value to me. I will be more likely to feel gratitude towards you—and more likely to invest in your idea, product, or service.

Likeability. We tend to purchase from those we like, as we've explored. In my networking groups, those who were authentically likable were the ones who received the most callbacks. As a speaker, trainer, and workshop facilitator,

I achieve better results if I take time getting to know the people in my audience before we start. The best way to secure likeability is to ask questions, and then listen to others talk.

Mirroring or Modeling. One way we as humans unconsciously decide if someone is trustworthy is by comparing that person to ourselves. Neuroscientists discovered a neuron called the mirror neuron which neuron fires whenever we do an action and someone else does a similar activity. Neuroscientists hypothesize that our brains have evolved so that when we see someone who acts like us, we feel a kinship. This is a technique used by salespeople worldwide to make you feel more comfortable around them. Ever noticed how, if you lean on a car while at the car dealership, the salesperson will do the same—or at least touch the vehicle? They are hoping this signals to you that you and the salesperson are the same.

Exercises to Improve Your Technique

- *Pull together all the social proof you have about your product, service, or idea—including client testimonials, case studies, and videos of a customer using your product.*

- *Create a value-add that you can give to potential clients for free.*

- *Practice mirroring a friend or family member. How do they respond? Do they keep the conversation going, or do they walk away? Try with strangers.*

- *Prepare messaging that creates a fear of missing out for your customers, clients, or boss.*

- *Build a membership portal that offers extras for those who sign up.*

Conclusion

Selling is the art and practice of influencing others to invest their money, time, energy, or prestige in your products, services, and ideas. It is something you do every day to some degree—whether at work, trying to influence your coworkers to start a new process, or at home, trying to influence your family members to clean the house you are selling.

Confession time—when I started as an entrepreneur, I sucked at selling. I sucked at selling, because in my mind's eye, I was afraid of the rejection that came with selling my product, services, and ideas. Here is the funny part: when I left the corporate world after twenty-five years, I had an operating budget of eight million dollars and three hundred and fifty staff members reporting up to me. Every day, I influenced others to invest in my ideas.

Still, I was afraid of the rejection that came with sales, and therefore, I never thought I would be good at selling a product, service, or ideas.

But I learned a secret: selling is a process. As described in this book, there are six steps you can practice, including *preparing to sell, connecting, influencing, being curious, sharing solutions*, and *closing the deal*. If you master all six, you will achieve your goals.

I never thought I would be good at selling. I did not believe I had the aptitude for selling myself, my ideas, my services, or my products.

But I did—and so do you!

Selling is essentially about building relationships, honoring the trust that people place in you, and providing your customers with value. If you do these three things well, you will be successful at sales.

My intention is for you to reference this book, time and time again. To be successful at any endeavor, you need confidence, a system, knowledge, and the ability to get it done. Use this book as your guide to achieving better performance. Actual improvement will come when you go to the market and start selling real customers on your ideas, products, and services. Ability can only come through *practice.*

But you can't just practice. You must practice with *intent.* Each day you go out and sell, have a *plan* and a *goal.* At the end of each day, go home and evaluate yourself.
Ask these three questions:

- *What did I do well?*

- *What did I not do well?*

- *What will I change in the future?*

If this simple self-assessment doesn't work, join one of my interactive on-line sales workshops, or hire me directly to be your sales coach. I wrote this book to guide you in achieving your dreams, yet I know from personal experience that going it alone doesn't always work. I found working with a coach to be beneficial to my career. My coach gave me guidance when I went astray, pushed me when I needed it, and celebrated with me in my success.

If you are interested in hiring me as a coach or having me work with your team to improve their sales techniques, reach out to me at: *salescoaching@johnthalheimer.com*

Good luck, and may you notice the many wonders of this world!

John

Resources

Chamandy, I., & Aber, K. (2015). *Why Should I Choose You? (in Seven Words or Less)*. New York NY: Harper Collins.

Cialdini, R. (2006). *Influence: The Psychology of Persuasion*. New York NY: William Morrow and Company.

Coleman, M. (2020). *Mike Coleman Marketing*. Retrieved from Mike Coleman Marketing: https://www.mikecoleman.net/

Dworak-Peck, S. (2020). *A Century of Smoking in Women's History*. Retrieved from Univesity of Southern California Nursing School: https://nursing.usc.edu/blog/womens-history-smoking/

Gardete, P. M. (2015). Fellow Airline Passengers Influence What You Buy. *Stanford Graduate School of Business*. Retrieved from www.gsb.stanford.edu/insights/pedro-m-gardete-fellow-airline-passengers-influence-what-you-buy

Patterson, K., Grenny, J., McMillian, R., & Switzler, A. (2012). *Crucial Conversations – Tools for Talking When Stakes are High*. New York, NY: McGraw Hill.

Rey, M. (1941). *Curious George*. New York, NY: Houghton Mifflin Company.

Salk, D. J. (1990, February 18). Jonas Salk on Searching for the Next Medical Miracle. (B. Mohr, Interviewer) Retrieved from https://billmoyers.com/content/jonas-salk/

Sesno, F. (2017). *Ask More*. New York, NY: American Management Association .

Strohmetz, D. B. (2002). Sweetening the Till: The Use of Candy to Increase Restaurant Tipping. *Journal of Applied Social Psychology, vol. 32*, 300-309.

University of Minnesota. (2010). *Principles of Marketing*. Minneapolis, MN: University of Minnesota Libraries Publishing .

Valin, S. V. (2019). *Culturology – Breakthrough from the inside out*. Retrieved from Culturology – Breakthrough from the inside out: Culturology – Breakthrough from the inside out

Zenger, J., & Folkman, J. (2016, July 14). What Great Listeners Actually Do. *Harvard Business Review*.

About the Author

I hated selling. The thought of asking someone to invest in my product, service, or idea was terrifying to me. I just didn't want to do it. It didn't help that the majority of small business owners and entrepreneurs responded with the same emotions.

Yet, after more than twenty-five years in the corporate world, I had enough people telling me what to do. So I started my own company, True Star Leadership™, offering practical advice to managers and supervisors to improve employees' performance. At first, I worked on building content, engaging leaders on social networking sites, and trying my hand at networking.

Like many entrepreneurs, I thought if I had a fantastic idea, clients would automatically come knocking at my door. They didn't.

I had to learn how to sell myself and my ideas, products, and services.

Luckily, I had one of the best learning grounds for selling. Having worked at QVC for over fifteen years, helping the on-air guests and program hosts prepare for on-air presentations, I learned how to influence customers, create urgency, ask the right questions, and practice the presentation.

Yet it wasn't until one of my clients asked me to take a commission-based training job that I started applying what I had learned. At first, I was horrible, with many weeks of zero dollars in sales. I realized that knowledge was different than ability. Each week, I worked on my sales techniques—practicing, changing, discovering what worked, and didn't work. There was no single guidebook for me to follow, but I created my own path.

I met many great salespeople along the way. I practiced active listening and asking the right questions to learn as much as possible. Most were generous with their time and energy. Some felt like magicians, sharing their techniques only to the highest bidder.

My sales got better.

For Christmas, I gave my wife tickets to a biscuit-making class. I did not know that decision would change my life. As I watched Mrs. Bryde teach us how to make biscuits—and the sales results she achieved at the end of the class—everything I had learned, practiced, and tried suddenly came together.

I knew what I must do.

Over the next month, I tweaked how I got people to invest in the necessary resources I offered. Slowly, my sales numbers increased, so that I became the number one salesperson for my client in two of my categories—and in the top five for all the rest. True Star Leadership™ sales doubled.

I was a successful salesperson.

And I didn't hate it.

Secretly, today, I might even like it just a little.

—*John Thalheimer*

Made in the USA
Coppell, TX
09 June 2021